Laugh
and the
Whole Church
Laughs with
You!

Publications International, Ltd.

Illustrator: Amanda Haley

Contributing Writers: Rebecca Christian, Kelly Cison, Lawrence Greenberg, Ellen Pill, Angela Sanchez, Terri Schlichenmeyer, Paul Seaburn, Kim Sloane, Carol Stigger, Niki Taylor, Lynda Twardowsky, Kathy Yonce

Louis Weber, CEO
Publications International, Ltd.
7373 North Cicero Avenue
Lincolnwood, Illinois 60712

ISBN-13: 978-1-4127-1768-7
ISBN-10: 1-4127-1768-4

Manufactured in USA.

8 7 6 5 4 3 2 1

It's not a sin to laugh in church...it's a sin not to!

Smiles are as contagious as yawns—but they're much more pleasing to your pastor. Joy and laughter can be found wherever you worship, from a church bulletin blooper to the unintended gaffe of an enthusiastic minister to the innocent words of a child in Sunday school. One smile lifts many spirits, so share a spiritual laugh today.

A new pastor moved into town and went out one Saturday to visit his parishioners. All went well until he came to one house. It was obvious that someone was home, but no one came to the door even after he had knocked several times. Finally, he took out his card, wrote on the back "Revelation 3:20" and stuck it in the door. ("Listen! I am standing at the door, knocking; if you hear my voice and open the door, I will come in to you and eat with you, and you with me.")

The next day, as the pastor was counting the offering, he found his card in the collection plate. Below his message was a notation "Genesis 3:10." ("He said, 'I heard the sound of you in the garden, and I was afraid, because I was naked; and I hid myself.'")

✳ ✳ ✳

Let us pray for Harold Johnson, who has been suffering from severe depression ever since joining our congregation.

Weekly church is God's gift. Assembly required.

✳ ✳ ✳

Dear God,

I went to this wedding and they kissed right in church. Is that okay?

Neil, age 8

CHURCH HAPPENINGS

Please join us for an all-you-can-eat dinner, followed by a sermon on gluttony by Father Bill.

✳ ✳ ✳

"The secret of a good sermon is to have a good beginning and a good ending; and to have the two as close together as possible."

GEORGE BURNS

A young pastor, fresh out of seminary, was invited to preach a sermon before the board of directors of a church to determine if she would be their new pastor. The directors liked the sermon very much, and they voted to bring the young pastor onboard. The next Sunday the young pastor preached the very same sermon to the congregation that she had to the directors. Although they thought it a bit odd, they decided not to mention it to her, thinking perhaps with the move to town she had not had time to prepare another one. The next Sunday, however, she delivered the exact same sermon, and this time a board meeting was called on Monday morning. An elder rose to speak, "Now see here, Pastor, we liked that sermon well enough to hire you, but you must tell us when you are going to preach a new one."

"Oh, certainly," the pastor nodded. "When it seems as though everyone understands the first one, then we'll move on to the next."

I'm from a country with no religion. So one day I saw a priest walking down the street. Noticing his collar, I stopped him and said, "Excuse me, but why are you wearing your shirt backward?"

The priest smiled benevolently, "Because, my son, I am a Father."

I scratched my head. "But I am a father too, and I don't wear my shirt backward!"

Again the priest laughed. "But I am a Father of thousands!"

To which I replied, "Well, then, you should wear your shorts backward!"

✳ ✳ ✳

Jesus cured Peter's mother-in-law when she was sick of a fever, and Peter swore and went out and wept bitterly.

CHURCH NEWS

The lecture on the religious history of circumcision has been cut from tonight's program.

❋ ❋ ❋

My wife and I invited several people to dinner. At the table, she turned to our eight-year-old daughter and said, "Would you like to say the blessing?"

"I wouldn't know what to say," she replied.

"Just say what you hear Mommy say," my wife encouraged. Our daughter bowed her head and said, "Dear Lord, why on earth did I invite all these people to dinner?"

9

God's Golf Game: Holy in One

✳ ✳ ✳

The preacher came to call on me the other day. He said that at my age I should be thinking about the hereafter. I told him I do—all time. No matter where I am, in the living room, upstairs in the kitchen, or down in the basement, I'm constantly asking myself, "Now, what am I here after?"

A man is struck by a bus on a busy street in New York City. He lies dying on the sidewalk as a crowd of spectators gathers around. "A priest. Somebody get me a priest!" the man gasps. A police officer surveys the crowd: no priest, no minister, no officer of God of any kind.

"A priest, *please!*" the dying man says again. Then out of the crowd steps an elderly Jewish man. "Officer," says the man. "I'm not a priest. I'm not even Catholic. But for 50 years now I've lived behind St. Elizabeth's Catholic Church on First Avenue, and every night I listen to the Catholic litany. So maybe I can be of some comfort to this poor dying man."

The police officer agrees, and he leads the old man over to where the dying man lies. The man kneels down, leans over the injured, and begins in a solemn voice, "B–4. I–19. N–38. G–54. O–72...."

A preacher received the offerings from the ushers and stared into the limp, velvet collection bag. He cleaned his glasses, looked in the bag again, then cleared his throat. He announced with the little enthusiasm he could muster, "Our mission to invite the poor to join our congregation has been an outstanding success. I can assure you they are all here."

※ ※ ※

CHURCH HAPPENINGS

Today's marital workshop, "Make Time for Your Marriage" has been canceled due to a scheduling conflict.

An atheist was spending a quiet day fishing when suddenly his boat was attacked by the Loch Ness monster. In one easy flip, the beast tossed him and his boat high into the air. Then it opened its mouth to swallow both.

As the man sailed head over heels, he cried out, "Oh, God! Help me!"

At once, the ferocious attack scene froze in place, and as the atheist hung in midair, a booming voice came down from the clouds, "I thought you didn't believe in me!"

"Come on, God, give me a break!" the man pleaded. "Two seconds ago I didn't believe in the Loch Ness monster either!"

✳ ✳ ✳

When asked to name a saint from the United States, Tia raised her hand and said, "Joan of Arkansas."

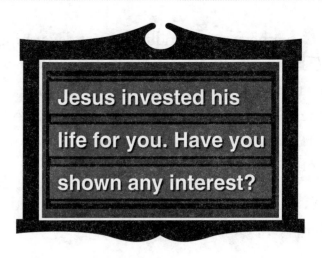

Jesus invested his life for you. Have you shown any interest?

❋ ❋ ❋

OUR CHURCH TODAY

A young woman was giving her testimony in church one night. "There have been so many wonderful changes in my life since I asked Jesus to live in my heart. Why, I was so angry at my father for so many years, I vowed I would never even go to his funeral. But now that I am a Christian, I would be delighted to go to his funeral anytime!"

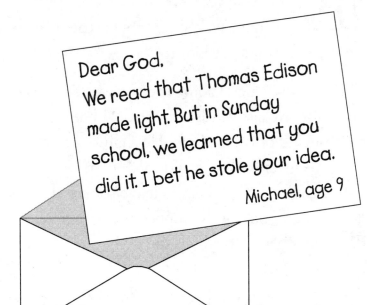

Dear God,
We read that Thomas Edison made light. But in Sunday school, we learned that you did it. I bet he stole your idea.

Michael, age 9

＊ ＊ ＊

Eight new choir robes are currently needed due to the addition of several new members and the deterioration of some of the older ones.

During the Reign of Terror, a rabbi, a priest, and a rationalist skeptic were on the docket for the morning's executions.

The rabbi was first. Facing the guillotine, he was asked for any last words and cried, "I believe in the one and only true God. He shall save me." The executioner then positioned the rabbi and pulled the cord. The heavy cleaver plunged downward but abruptly stopped inches above the rabbi's neck. To which the rabbi said, "I told you so."

"A miracle!" gasped the crowd. The executioner agreed and let the rabbi go free.

Next was the priest. Asked for final words, he declared, "I believe in Jesus Christ the Father, Son, and Holy Ghost who will rescue me in my hour of need." The executioner positioned him and pulled the cord. Again the blade flew downward and again stopped just short.

"Another miracle!" sighed the crowd. The executioner again let the condemned go.

Now it was the skeptic's turn. "What final words do you have?" he was asked. But he didn't hear, as he was staring intently at the guillotine. Not until the executioner poked him and the question was asked again did he reply.

"I see your problem," the skeptic said, pointing. "There's a blockage in the gear assembly, right there!"

※　※　※

The Browns invited their pastor for dinner. As he took his seat, he asked the family if he might say a prayer before the meal was served.

Before his parents could answer, little Johnny piped up, "No need to pray, Pastor Thomas—Mom's a great cook!"

Mrs. Davis paused as she shook the pastor's hand when leaving church one Sunday morning. "That was a wonderful sermon, Pastor. I would love it if you had all of your sermons printed up, so we could take them home and study them."

"Thank you so much, Mrs. Davis. As a matter of fact, I do intend to have many of my sermons published posthumously."

"Oh, that's good news," Mrs. Davis effused. "The sooner the better."

❋ ❋ ❋

CHURCH NOTES

Do you love to sin? The church choir is looking for new members.

A small midwestern town was in the midst of a long drought, and all the farmers were in fear of losing their crops. At church on Sunday, the pastor led them in a fervent prayer asking the Lord for rain. He closed out the service by instructing his flock to spend the whole week in prayer for rain and to come back next Sunday  morning prepared to thank the Lord for answered prayers. By the next Sunday morning, it still had not rained, and the church was full. The pastor stood at the pulpit, looked out over the congregation, and shook his head sadly. He accused the people of not believing in the Lord.

"We do believe," they all protested.

"Then where are your umbrellas?" he asked.

Dear Pastor,
Will the Book of Job help me find one?

Sheila, age 17

※ ※ ※

CHURCH NOTES

WANTED: Volunteer Sunday school teacher, casserole baker, nursery worker, janitor, fund-raiser, receptionist, nurse, and piano player—in other words, pastor's wife.

✳ ✳ ✳

Marisol and her mother were walking home from church one Sunday morning, and Marisol looked up at her mother. "Mommy, something the Reverend said confuses me. He said that God is bigger than us, and he is bigger than all our problems. He also said that God can live in my heart. Won't he come poking out?"

Joshua went to see his rabbi. "I need your advice. The doctor just told my wife and me we will be having a boy."

"Mazel tov," exclaimed the rabbi.

"Thank you, Rabbi. As you might expect, we are hoping to name the baby after a relative."

The rabbi nodded. Of course, in accordance with Jewish custom, they might name a baby after a departed father, mother, brother...

"But they're all still living," said Joshua.

"That's too bad," said the rabbi. "When is the baby due?"

"In four months," answered Joshua.

The rabbi shook his head. "Well, we can only hope...."

✳ ✳ ✳

Father John turned beet red when he turned to the newly married groom and said, "You may now kick the bride."

Dear Pastor,
If Sarah was 90 and Abraham was 100 when they had Isaac, who drove him to soccer practice?

Sophie, age 8

❋ ❋ ❋

A little boy walked up to his father and asked him, "Daddy, how do you spell God?" The father replied, "G-O-D." The boy wrote it down, then turned to his father once more and asked, "Now how do you spell 'Zilla?"

As the wedding began, the little boy had to go to the bathroom, but his mom kept asking him to hold it. All was well until the minister declared, "Speak now, or forever hold your peace." At that point, the little boy said urgently to his mom: "I can't hold it *forever!*"

✳ ✳ ✳

Preacher D. L. Moody had been forewarned that some of the congregation usually left before the end of the sermon. When he rose to begin his sermon, he led by saying, "I am going to speak to two groups of people this morning; first to the sinners among us, then to the saints." After the first part of the sermon, he looked around and told the "sinners" they could leave. For once, every member of the church stayed to the end of the sermon.

Searching for a new look? Have your faith lifted here!

* * *

THIS WEEK'S SERMON

One beautiful Sunday morning, a priest announced to his congregation: "Friends, I have here in my hands three sermons... a $100 sermon that lasts five minutes, a $50 sermon that lasts fifteen minutes, and a $10 sermon that lasts a full hour. Now, we'll take the collection and see which one I'll deliver."

George W. Bush was walking through a hotel lobby when he noticed a man in a long, flowing, white robe with a long, flowing, white beard and long, flowing, white hair. The man had a staff in one hand and some stone tablets under his other arm.

Struck by the man's appearance, George W. approached the man and whispered, "Aren't you Moses?"

The man stood perfectly still and continued to stare at the ceiling, saying nothing.

George W., unaccustomed to being ignored, positioned himself more directly in the man's view. He asked again, "Aren't you Moses?"

The man resolutely stared up at the ceiling.

George W. then tugged at the man's sleeve and demanded, "Well, are you Moses or not?"

Again, there was no movement or words from the old man.

One of George W.'s aides asked if there was a problem, and George W. said, "Either this man is deaf or he's extremely rude. I've asked him three times if he's Moses, and he hasn't answered me yet."

At this point, the man finally responded, turning to the aide and saying, "Yes, I can hear him and yes, I am Moses, but the last time I spoke to a bush I ended up wandering in the desert for 40 years."

✳ ✳ ✳

"Adam blamed Eve, Eve blamed the serpent, and the serpent didn't have a leg to stand on."

A producer, a grip, and a director riding in the grip truck were involved in a horrible traffic accident. They all died and went to heaven.

When they knocked on the Pearly Gates, St. Peter appeared and asked for their names and occupations. Then he said, "Listen, fellas, I'm seriously overloaded here right now. Tell you what— if each of you gives me ten dollars, I'll send you back to live out your natural lives, and you can come back peacefully, when I'm not so busy."

As soon as the director heard this, she pulled a tenner out of her wallet and handed it to the saint. Shortly thereafter, she came to her senses in the wreckage of the truck, with a police officer peering in. After pulling her out of the wrecked truck and helping her to the side of the road, the officer asked what had happened. The director told him all about the experience with St. Peter at the gates of heaven.

The cop looked around and asked what happened to the other two chaps.

"I'm not sure," said the director. "When I left, the producer had him negotiated down to $8.50 and the grip was looking for a cosigner."

※ ※ ※

A pastor asked a little boy if he said his prayers every night.

"Yes, sir," the boy replied.

"And, do you always say them in the morning too?" the pastor asked.

"No, sir," the boy replied. "I'm not scared in the daytime."

Things you never hear in church...

1. Hey! It's my turn to sit in the front pew.

2. I was so enthralled, I never noticed the sermon ran 25 minutes long.

3. Personally, I find witnessing much more enjoyable than golf.

4. I've decided to give our church the $500 a month I used to send to TV evangelists.

5. I volunteer to be the permanent teacher for the junior high Sunday school class.

6. I love it when we sing hymns I've never heard before.

7. Since we're all here, let's start the service early.

8. Pastor, we'd like to send you to a Bible seminar in the Bahamas.

9. Nothing inspires me and strengthens my commitment like our annual stewardship campaign.

10. I couldn't find space to park outside. Praise God!

CHURCH

NEWS

The associate minister unveiled the church's new tithing campaign slogan last Sunday: "I Upped My Pledge—Up Yours."

✳ ✳ ✳

ACKNOWLEDGMENTS

The "Over-Sixties" choir will disband for the winter with the thanks of the entire church.

CHURCH HAPPENINGS

Anyone who has lost their job recently is invited to attend a special service on Monday evening to join together and pray to a hire power.

❋ ❋ ❋

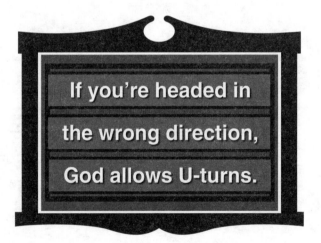

If you're headed in the wrong direction, God allows U-turns.

A young boy wanted a bicycle very badly. His parents couldn't afford to buy him one, so every night, with all the faith he could muster, he prayed for God to bring him one. Months went by, and he didn't get his bike, but he was learning more and more about the Lord. He finally gave up praying for one.

The next day his mother was stunned to see him come home from school on a very nice bike. She demanded to know where he got it.

"I stole it, Mama," he answered. "But don't worry. Tonight when I pray I'm going to ask for forgiveness."

Jesus, Moses, and an elderly man are playing golf. Moses steps up to the tee and hits the ball. It goes sailing over the fairway and lands in the water trap. So Moses parts the water and chips onto the green.

Jesus steps up to the tee and hits the ball. It too goes sailing over the fairway and lands in the water trap. Jesus just walks on the water and chips the ball onto the green.

Next, the old man steps up to the tee and hits the ball. It goes sailing over the fairway and heads for the water trap. But just before it lands in the water a fish jumps up and catches the ball in his mouth, then an eagle swoops down and grabs the fish in its claws. The eagle flies over the green and is hit by a sudden bolt of lightning, dropping the fish. When the fish hits the ground, the ball pops out of its mouth and rolls in for a hole in one.

Jesus then turns to the old man and says, "Dad, if you don't stop showing off we won't bring you next time!"

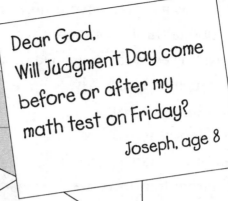

Dear God,
Will Judgment Day come before or after my math test on Friday?

Joseph, age 8

CHURCH NOTES

SLINGSHOT: $10.

ROCK: Free.

CHANCE TO SAVE YOUR PEOPLE FROM A GIANT: Priceless.

Sister Mary was a devout nun who had served God faithfully for more than 50 years. Lately, however, the years had begun to show in her memory. Recently, on a train to go visit a nun who was in the hospital, Sister Mary began to look rather frantic as she searched for her ticket. The conductor came over and, realizing she had lost her ticket, assured her he

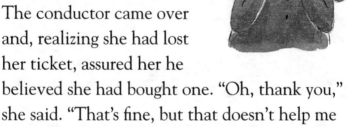

believed she had bought one. "Oh, thank you," she said. "That's fine, but that doesn't help me know where I'm going, now does it?"

✳ ✳ ✳

The sermon had droned on for nearly two hours. Finally, the minister stretched his arms out wide and asked, "What more can I say?" To which a teenager sitting in the back called out, "'Amen' would be nice."

CHURCH

NEWS

Congratulations to our Children's Choir for winning second place at the Community Sing. Dressed as angels, they tinkled like stars.

※ ※ ※

CHURCH HAPPENINGS

At the church picnic, the ladies will bring side dishes. The Men's Fellowship will barbecue a pig provided by the Ruiz family. Jim and Ted Macquarie have offered to turn the rotisserie, and Ted Fawns will boast.

After creating heaven and earth, God created Adam and Eve. And the first thing he said to them was, "Don't."

"Don't what?" Adam asked.

"Don't eat the forbidden fruit," God said.

"Forbidden fruit? We got forbidden fruit? Hey, Eve! We got forbidden fruit!"

"No way!"

"Yes way!"

"Don't eat that fruit!" said God.

"Why?"

"Because I'm your Creator and I said so!" said God.

A few minutes later, God saw the kids having an apple break, and he became very angry. "Didn't I tell you not to eat that fruit?" God asked.

"Uh-huh," Adam replied.

"Then why did you eat it?"

"I dunno," Eve answered.

"She started it!" Adam said.

"Did not!"

"Did so!"

"Did not!"

Having had it with the two of them, God vowed that their punishment would be that they would have children of their own.

Our senior pastor was a reservist in the U.S. Marines, and he was called up last year to serve as a chaplin in Iraq. He left our church in the hands of his eldest son, who was the youth pastor and a very capable young man. Nevertheless, it gave our pastor some concern when he received this note from a member of the congregation:

Dear Pastor,
We are praying for you and your unit. The church misses you. Your son is carrying on with the choir. It is really something.

✳ ✳ ✳

"I'm glad Moses wasn't a weight lifter," said little Laurel, "or he might have carried a lot more stone tablets covered with commandments."

No God: No Peace.

Know God:

Know Peace.

❋ ❋ ❋

CHURCH NOTES

The men's prayer breakfast will be held
Wednesday at 8:00 A.M. No charge,
but your damnation will be gratefully
accepted.

An avid golfer gets a once-in-a-lifetime chance for an audience with the pope. After standing in line for hours, he gets to the pope and says, "Holiness, I have a question that only you can answer. Is there a golf course in heaven?"

The pope considers for a moment, then says, "I do not know the answer to your question, my son, but I will talk to God and get back to you."

The next day the man is called for another audience with the pope to receive the answer to his question. He stands before the pope, who says, "I have some good news and some bad news for you. The good news is that heaven has the most fabulous golf course that you could imagine, and it is in eternally perfect shape."

"And what's the bad news?" asks the man.

"You tee off tomorrow morning," the pope replies.

CHURCH HAPPENINGS

After the service, a young man overheard the priest say the morning's collection didn't bring in as much as the parish needed. The young man nudged the priest: "Have you tried serving more wine?"

❋ ❋ ❋

Dear Pastor,
I don't understand why all religions can't get along. The priests, rabbis, and ministers in Daddy's jokes always seem to have a lot of fun together.

Colby, age 9

On the way to church one Sunday morning, Johnny's mother turned to him and asked if he understood why it was important to be quiet during the service.

"Yes, Mommy, I know. Because Daddy will be asleep."

✳ ✳ ✳

CHURCH NOTES

Only a small number of deceased elders have been sent to us. You can still bring yours to the meeting to be added to the list.

CHURCH HAPPENINGS

While the Ladies' Club meets to work on their quilts, husbands are invited to hear a talk entitled "Be not afraid, thy Comforter is coming."

✳ ✳ ✳

A Sunday school teacher decided to have her young class memorize one of the most quoted passages in the Bible: Psalm 23. She gave the youngsters a month to learn the chapter. Ricky was excited about the task, but he just couldn't remember the psalm. After much practice, he still could barely get past the first line. On the day that the kids were scheduled to recite the psalm in front of the congregation, Ricky was nervous. When it was his turn, he stepped up to the microphone and said proudly, "The Lord is my Shepherd, and that's all I need to know."

Don't let worry kill you. The Church can help.

✳ ✳ ✳

When the missionary shouldered his rifle as he left on his journey for some of the more remote villages of Africa, the church members questioned him. "Don't you trust in the Lord, young man?"

"Of course I do. I am taking this in case I meet a lion or a leopard that believes in him also."

The members looked puzzled.

The missionary patiently explained, "I mean one who believes the Lord has just provided him with dinner."

THIS WEEK'S

Reverend Bob reassured the older men in the congregation, "If Samson were alive today, he'd probably have a bald spot too."

❋ ❋ ❋

CHURCH NOTES

Anyone wishing to join our new singles group should put their name on a card and drop it in the connection basket.

The three wise men arrived to visit the child in the manger. One of the wise men was exceptionally tall, and he bumped his head on the low doorway as he entered the stable. "Jesus Christ!" he exclaimed, rubbing his head.

Joseph said, "Write that down, Mary; it's a lot better than Stanley!"

Bible Lessons

AMEN: The only part of a prayer that everyone knows.

HOLY WATER: A liquid whose chemical formula is H_2OLY.

INCENSE: Holy Smoke!

MAGI: The most famous trio to attend a baby shower.

PROCESSIONAL: The ceremonial formation at the beginning of Mass, consisting of altar servers, the celebrant, and late parishioners looking for seats.

RECESSIONAL: The ceremonial procession at the conclusion of Mass, led by parishioners trying to beat the crowd to the parking lot.

A Sunday school teacher asked, "Michael, do you think Noah did a lot of fishing when he was on the ark?"

"No," replied Michael. "How could he, with just two worms?"

* * *

CHURCH HAPPENINGS

Would all the anonymous group members in the congregation please raise their hands concerning the 12-step fund-raiser?

* * *

Reverend Calvin's mother runs a gas station. One row of pumps has a sign that says, "Full service." The other row of pumps says, "God helps those who help themselves."

A pastor paid a visit to a member of his congregation who was recuperating in the hospital. As the doctor was leaving the patient's room, she explained that because Roy was on some potent pain medication, she and the other doctors on call had been asking him questions to determine if he was disoriented.

"So, how are you doing?" the pastor asked Roy.

"I'm feeling fine," Roy answered, "but I don't think much of these young doctors. Not a one of 'em knows who the president is."

✳ ✳ ✳

"No one ever asked Jesus to help them move," said Tim, "because Jesus would have said, 'Rise, take up thy bed and walk.'"

Edith was the church gossip, spreading rumors to groups of congregants by asking for prayers for "so and so, who were arguing in the store. . . ." She was always on the lookout for "news," substantiated or not.

Sam was new to church, and he kept to himself a lot, so Edith was having a tough time getting any goods on him. Finally one Saturday afternoon she noticed Sam's truck in front of the town's bar, and she could barely sleep that night she was so thrilled with her discovery.

The next morning, she spread the word that people should pray for Sam to find the road to recovery, for he had a drinking problem. In fact, she offered Sam prayer as he was seated in the sanctuary, just loud enough so that at least four rows around him clearly heard her "concerns" for his addiction to the bottle. Sam sat silently and listened to her.

And later that night he quietly parked his pickup truck in front of Edith's house and left it there all night.

Dear God,
I heard about how Jesus turned water into wine. Did you know my mom can turn water into Kool-Aid?

Andrew, age 6

* * *

Ad in bulletin for auto repair service:

Amazing Grace Body Shop:
We Save Wrecks
Like Yours

A father brought his daughter to church. He sat in the very front row so that she could properly witness the service. During this particular service, the minister was performing the baptism of a tiny infant. The little girl was taken by  this, observing that he was saying something and pouring water over the infant's head. Turning to her father, she asked, "Daddy, why is he brainwashing that baby?"

✳ ✳ ✳

CHURCH HAPPENINGS

For next week's men's clothing drive, we are requesting you drop your pants in the foyer.

THIS WEEK'S

SERMON

When asked about the fallen angels, Reverend Tim, a baseball fan, said, "The Angels may have fallen, but they can still beat the Mariners this weekend."

✳ ✳ ✳

CHURCH NOTES

A cookbook is being compiled by the ladies of the church. Please submit your favorite recipe, along with a short antidote for it.

Four boys ages 8 to 12 stood outside the church arguing just before the pastor was to perform a funeral.

"Come, now, fellows," said the pastor. "I can't have this ruckus out here during Mr. Collins's memorial service. What's the problem?"

One of the boys spoke up, "It's like this. We all want Mr. Collins's good old hunting dog. We have to come up with a way to settle who will get Ol' Red, so we've decided that the one who can tell the best lie wins him."

"Oh no, boys," the pastor looked shocked. "That idea is straight from the pit of hell. Why, when I was your age, I never told a single lie."

The boys stood silently, looking around at each other. The same boy spoke for the group. "All right, Pastor, you win."

Bible Lessons

CHOIR: A group of people whose singing allows the rest of the congregation to lip-synch.

RECESSIONAL HYMN: The last song at a service, often sung a little more quietly, since most of the people have already left.

JONAH: The original *Jaws* story.

PEW: A medieval torture device still found in churches.

RELICS: People who have been going to Mass for so long, they actually know when to sit, kneel, and stand.

USHERS: The only people in the parish who don't know the seating capacity of a pew.

Mike had never missed a chance to serve the Lord his entire adult life. He didn't drink, gamble, or cheat. Lately, though, he found himself going through hard times.

"Lord, please, I am in deep trouble. I never thought I would ask for something like this, but please, Lord, let me win the lottery, just this once." Mike continued to pray, but lotto drawings came and went and he did not win.

"Lord, why have you forsaken me? I desperately need this, or I'll lose my home, my car, my wife. Please Lord, I will never gamble again." He continued to pray desperately, but it seemed as though the Lord had turned his back.

Finally the Lord answered Mike audibly, "Truly, my son, you have been a good and faithful servant, so I have chosen to bless this unusual petition. However, Mike, please, BUY A TICKET!"

Sign at a Christian music shop:

What Would Jesus Dig?

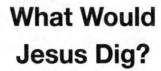

* * *

CHURCH

Indulge your sweet tooth!
Everything purchased at
the annual bake sale will go
directly into the church's new
plumbing system.

I n a cemetery outside of town stands an old pecan tree. One day, two boys had filled a bucket with nuts and sat down to divide them between themselves. "One for you, one for me. One for you, one for me," said one boy. A few pecans dropped and rolled down toward the fence.

Another boy came riding along the road on his bicycle. As he passed the cemetery, he heard the voices and stopped to listen.

"One for you, one for me. One for you, one for me. One for..."

He was just about to take off when an elderly man came hobbling along. "Come here!" said the boy. "You won't believe what I heard! Satan and the Lord are down at the cemetery dividing up the souls."

The man shuffled over to the fence. They heard the voices again, "One for you, one for me. One for you, one for me."

"By golly, boy, you were right! Let's get a little closer, and maybe we can see the Lord."

But the next thing they heard was, "That's all for now. Let's go get those nuts by the fence, and we'll be done."

The boy couldn't keep up with the old man as they raced back to town.

❋ ❋ ❋

CHURCH NOTES

The potluck supper raised $850 for missions. Whoever left bowls, plates, and a girdle in the kitchen, please retrieve your personal items.

A church preschool teacher was watching her class of four-year-olds enjoying free time for art. One little girl seemed especially engrossed in her drawing, so the teacher walked over to take a closer look.

"I'm drawing a picture of God," said Callie.

"Oh, honey, no one knows what God looks like," said the teacher.

"Well, they will when I'm done!" replied Callie.

Sign in a restaurant window:

**HELP WANTED.
Blessed is he
that waiteth.**
DAN. 12:12

A woman was so enthralled while hiking in the Grand Canyon that she completely forgot to be cautious and slipped off a dangerous trail. As she slipped, she managed to grasp a branch sticking out from the wall of the cliff. "Please, Jesus, there is no help in sight, and I can't hold on for long. Help me, Jesus, please!"

"Certainly, I'll help you," she heard. "Just prove your faith by letting go of the branch."

The woman looked down at the 300-foot drop below her, and answered, "Could I speak with your dad, please?"

✳ ✳ ✳

The Catholic school nuns were horrified by the students' dirty mouths. For punishment, the kids had to clean the school bathrooms until not even one speck of grime was visible—what the nuns referred to as "immaculate perception."

One morning a fellow finds himself standing at the Pearly Gates. St. Peter explains that it's not easy to get into heaven. There are some criteria that must be met before entry is allowed. For example, was the man a churchgoer?

No? St. Peter tells him that's not good.

Was he generous, giving money to the poor or to charities?

No? St. Peter tells him this, too, is bad.

Did he do any good deeds, such as helping his neighbor? Anything? No? St. Peter is becoming concerned.

Exasperated, he says, "Look, everybody does something nice sometime. Work with me—I'm trying to help. Think!'"

The man thinks for a minute, then says, "Oh—I did help this old lady once. I came out of a store and saw that a dozen Hell's Angels had taken her purse and were shoving her around. I threw my bags down and got her purse back, then I

called the biggest biker a coward and spat in his face."

St. Peter is impressed. "When did this happen?" he asks.

"Oh, about 15 minutes ago," the man replied.

※ ※ ※

"The first time I sang in the church choir, two hundred people changed their religion."

FRED ALLEN

A Sunday school teacher was telling her students the story of the Good Samaritan. She asked them, "If you saw a person lying on the roadside, wounded and bleeding, what would you do?"

A thoughtful little girl broke the hushed silence, "I think I'd throw up."

✳ ✳ ✳

CHURCH NOTES

When the pastor finishes today's sermon, please join us in singing "Joy to the World."

OUR CHURCH TODAY

Father Dan got football fans to attend Sunday services by promising a "two-minute drill" sermon.

❋ ❋ ❋

The Huron River flows through the town of Ypsilanti, Michigan, a town with many small, evangelical churches. In one of these churches, a congregant found Jesus and became so involved in his newfound faith that he wanted to share it with everyone. He shared it, all right. His favorite testimony became: "Thank the Lord for saving my soul and baptizing me in the Urine River."

A preacher's little boy inquired, "Daddy, every Sunday when you first come out to preach, you sit on the platform and bow your head. What are you doing?"

The father explained, "I'm asking the Lord to give me a good sermon."

The little boy asked, "Why doesn't he?"

✳ ✳ ✳

OUR CHURCH TODAY

The Sunday school teacher could tell it was getting close to lunchtime when Roger asked her to tell the class about the multiplication of the French fries and fish sandwiches.

CHURCH NOTES

Remember the children's ministry bake sale. Our kids make great snacks.

✳ ✳ ✳

A woman goes repeatedly to her doctor, requesting new pills to help her feel better. He has given her every type of mood lifter he is able to prescribe and then finally, realizing that they are members of the same church, recommends she go to speak with their pastor.

"Pastor, please, I have tried every type of pill there is, but nothing makes me feel better. Can you help?" she pleaded.

"Certainly," he answered. "I have something that will help you if you use it daily. It's straight from the Lord, and it's called the Goss-Pill!"

After Seamus attended his first christening ceremony with his parents, he asked them, "Why didn't they talk about the mommy? They talked about the daddy, the baby, and the priest!"

"They did?" his mother asked.

"Well, they said 'in the name of the father, the son, and the Holy Host!'"

* * *

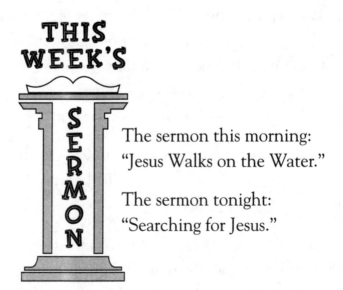

THIS WEEK'S SERMON

The sermon this morning: "Jesus Walks on the Water."

The sermon tonight: "Searching for Jesus."

Reverend Bob complimented the ladies in the congregation on their dress but cautioned them with a smile that if someone else didn't like their fashion tastes, they should "turn the other chic."

✳ ✳ ✳

A little girl, dressed in her Sunday best, was running as fast as she could, trying not to be late for Bible class.

As she ran she prayed, "Dear Lord, please don't let me be late! Dear Lord, please don't let me be late!"

As she was running, she tripped on a curb and fell, getting her clothes dirty and tearing her dress. She got up, brushed herself off, and started running again.

As she ran, she once again began to pray, "Dear Lord, please don't let me be late! But don't shove me either."

Bible Lessons

BULLETIN: 1. Parish information read only during the sermon. **2.** Catholic air-conditioning. **3.** Your receipt for attending the service.

HYMN: A song of praise, usually sung in a key three octaves higher than that of the congregation's range.

JESUITS: An order of priests known for their ability to found colleges with good basketball teams.

MANGER: 1. Where Mary gave birth to Jesus because Joseph wasn't covered by an HMO. **2.** The Bible's way of showing us that holiday travel has always been rough.

TEN COMMANDMENTS: The most important Top Ten list not given by David Letterman.

CHURCH NOTES

We need volunteers for summer camp. There will be sinning and dancing.

✳ ✳ ✳

Lynn spent the entire ride home from church inspecting the bottom of her shoe. She finally put it back on and told her mom, "I know why Reverend Ron told us to do some sole searching. I found gum, tape, and a bug on mine!"

"Why do we always sing about food at church?" the little boy asked his grandma.

"I can't think of any hymns with food in them," she answered.

Her grandson persisted, "Well, what about 'Sleep in Heavenly Peas' and 'Up From the Gravy, A Rose?'"

Dear Pastor,
My father says I should learn the Ten Commandments. But I don't think I want to because we already have enough rules in our house.

Chrissy, age 6

The priest discovered that two of his teenage parishioners had been gambling and drinking. When he called them into his office, they confessed. The priest thought for a moment about how to punish them for their sins, then went to the parish kitchen and returned with two cups of dried peas. He gave each teen one cup, with these instructions: "Divide these peas into your shoes and walk on them for a week to remind yourselves how hard life can be when you turn away from God."

A few days later, the two students met each other in the street. One was limping, looking miserable, while the other seemed none the worse for the punishment. "How is it that your feet don't even hurt? Didn't you do as Father instructed and put the peas in your shoes?" inquired the first teen.

"I did," said the other. "But I boiled them first."

CHURCH NOTES

For those of you who have children and don't know it, we have a nursery downstairs.

☀ ☀ ☀

Saul knew he had moved to a heavily Christian town when he was watching the *Star Wars* trilogy at the local movie theater. Every time the phrase "May the force be with you," was uttered on-screen, the audience replied, "And also with you."

The senior pastor and his youth pastor found a great fishing spot created by a tree downed in a recent storm. Before they began to fish, though, they made a large sign and taped it to the back of the pastor's truck: "The end is near! Stop! Make a U-turn before it's too late!"

When a car drove by the pastors pointed at the sign and shouted at the driver, to no avail. The driver slowed down and hollered back, "You religious nuts drive me crazy. Mind your own business!" A moment later they heard a loud splash. The senior pastor looked at his friend and asked, "Do you think we should have just written 'Bridge Out' on the sign?"

OUR CHURCH TODAY

I once asked my third grade Sunday school class to stand up and share, in just one sentence, "What Easter means to me." Some of the answers were sweet and some poignant, however, this is the one I remember the most:

"Egg salad sandwiches for the entire week."

THIS WEEK'S SERMON

The Gospel according to Luck

When Lucy's philosophy professor discovered she was a Christian, he targeted her for debate. She more than held her own, however.

He asked her to explain to him how any book could possibly be taken seriously that claims a man could stay alive in the belly of a giant fish for three days.

"I can't explain that, sir," Lucy answered. "However, when I get to heaven, I will ask Jonah myself how it was accomplished."

"And if Jonah isn't in heaven?" challenged the professor.

"Well, sir, then I suppose you can ask him yourself."

Let us pray for the teens in our church who will spend their summer at Bible Camp.

The nervous young pastor had taken over the church just weeks before one of the most distinguished members had passed on to glory. Wanting to make a good impression and knowing there would be a large turnout for the funeral, the pastor worked long and hard on his notes for the service. He was doing very well, until he reached what he thought would be a very meaningful analogy: "The body of a Christian is like that of an almond." He pointed to the casket and said, "The body is only the shell, and our dear friend, the nut, has already gone on..."